MAD LIBS®

DOG ATE MY MAD LIBS

Mad Libs
An Imprint of Penguin Random House

MAD LIBS
Penguin Young Readers Group
An Imprint of Penguin Random House LLC

Mad Libs format and text copyright © 2015 by Penguin Random House LLC. All rights reserved.

Concept created by Roger Price & Leonard Stern

Photo credit: cover, page 1: (Pug 17 months) © Thinkstock, photo by Eric Isselée

Published by Mad Libs,
an imprint of Penguin Random House LLC,
345 Hudson Street, New York, New York 10014.
Printed in the USA.

ISBN 9780843182934

MAD LIBS®
INSTRUCTIONS

MAD LIBS® is a game for people who don't like games! It can be played by one, two, three, four, or forty.

● RIDICULOUSLY SIMPLE DIRECTIONS

In this tablet you will find stories containing blank spaces where words are left out. One player, the READER, selects one of these stories. The READER does not tell anyone what the story is about. Instead, he/she asks the other players, the WRITERS, to give him/her words. These words are used to fill in the blank spaces in the story.

● TO PLAY

The READER asks each WRITER in turn to call out a word—an adjective or a noun or whatever the space calls for—and uses them to fill in the blank spaces in the story. The result is a MAD LIBS® game.

When the READER then reads the completed MAD LIBS® game to the other players, they will discover that they have written a story that is fantastic, screamingly funny, shocking, silly, crazy, or just plain dumb—depending upon which words each WRITER called out.

● EXAMPLE (*Before* and *After*)

" _____ !" he said _____
        EXCLAMATION   ADVERB

as he jumped into his convertible _____ and
                                              NOUN

drove off with his _____ wife.
                          ADJECTIVE

" _____*Ouch*_____ !" he said _____*stupidly*_____
        EXCLAMATION   ADVERB

as he jumped into his convertible _____*cat*_____ and
                                              NOUN

drove off with his _____*brave*_____ wife.
                          ADJECTIVE

In case you have forgotten what adjectives, adverbs, nouns, and verbs are, here is a quick review:

An ADJECTIVE describes something or somebody. *Lumpy, soft, ugly, messy,* and *short* are adjectives.

An ADVERB tells how something is done. It modifies a verb and usually ends in "ly." *Modestly, stupidly, greedily,* and *carefully* are adverbs.

A NOUN is the name of a person, place, or thing. *Sidewalk, umbrella, bridle, bathtub,* and *nose* are nouns.

A VERB is an action word. *Run, pitch, jump,* and *swim* are verbs. Put the verbs in past tense if the directions say PAST TENSE. *Ran, pitched, jumped,* and *swam* are verbs in the past tense.

When we ask for A PLACE, we mean any sort of place: a country or city (*Spain, Cleveland*) or a room (*bathroom, kitchen*).

An EXCLAMATION or SILLY WORD is any sort of funny sound, gasp, grunt, or outcry, like *Wow!, Ouch!, Whomp!, Ick!,* and *Gadzooks!*

When we ask for specific words, like a NUMBER, a COLOR, an ANIMAL, or a PART OF THE BODY, we mean a word that is one of those things, like *seven, blue, horse,* or *head.*

When we ask for a PLURAL, it means more than one. For example, *cat* pluralized is *cats.*

MAD LIBS® is fun to play with friends, but you can also play it by yourself! To begin with, DO NOT look at the story on the page below. Fill in the blanks on this page with the words called for. Then, using the words you have selected, fill in the blank spaces in the story.

Now you've created your own hilarious MAD LIBS® game!

DOG DAYS

VERB ENDING IN "ING" _____

PART OF THE BODY _____

PLURAL NOUN _____

VERB _____

NOUN _____

A PLACE _____

ADVERB _____

NOUN _____

PLURAL NOUN _____

PART OF THE BODY _____

PART OF THE BODY _____

PLURAL NOUN _____

PLURAL NOUN _____

NOUN _____

MAD LIBS

DOG DAYS

Have you always wondered what it's like to be a dog?

7:00 a.m.: I wake up and my tummy is _____.
<u>VERB ENDING IN "ING"</u> I bug my

human by licking her _____ until I get some _____
<u>PART OF THE BODY</u> <u>PLURAL NOUN</u>

7:30 a.m.: Potty time! My human takes me outside to _____
<u>VERB</u>

on a/an _____.
<u>NOUN</u>

8:00 a.m.: My human leaves to go to (the) _____. I am sad
<u>A PLACE</u>

and pout _____.
<u>ADVERB</u>

9:00 a.m.: Naptime. I cuddle on my favorite _____ and dream
<u>NOUN</u>

about chasing _____.
<u>PLURAL NOUN</u>

6:00 p.m.: MY HUMAN IS HOME! FINALLY! I wag my

_____ back and forth, and give my human kisses on the
<u>PART OF THE BODY</u>

_____.
<u>PART OF THE BODY</u>

6:30 p.m.: My human takes me for a walk, and I sniff lots of

_____.
<u>PLURAL NOUN</u>

7:00 p.m.: Dinnertime! Eating _____ is my favorite!
<u>PLURAL NOUN</u>

9:00 p.m.: I snuggle up next to my human and fall asleep, happy as

a/an _____.
<u>NOUN</u>

From DOG ATE MY MAD LIBS® • Copyright © 2015 by Penguin Random House LLC.

MAD LIBS® is fun to play with friends, but you can also play it by yourself! To begin with, DO NOT look at the story on the page below. Fill in the blanks on this page with the words called for. Then, using the words you have selected, fill in the blank spaces in the story.

Now you've created your own hilarious MAD LIBS® game!

WHO'S THAT DOG?, PART 1

A PLACE _____

NOUN _____

PLURAL NOUN _____

VERB _____

VERB ENDING IN "ING" _____

ADJECTIVE _____

ADJECTIVE _____

ADJECTIVE _____

NOUN _____

ADJECTIVE _____

ADJECTIVE _____

VERB _____

A PLACE _____

NOUN _____

MAD LIBS
WHO'S THAT DOG?, PART 1

With hundreds of breeds of dogs in (the) _____, there's one
A PLACE

for every kind of _____. Here are a few popular breeds:
NOUN

Golden retriever: The golden retriever is one of the most popular family

_____. Intelligent and eager to _____, the golden
PLURAL NOUN _VERB_

retriever makes an excellent _____ companion, and
VERB ENDING IN "ING"

is also a/an _____ guide dog.
ADJECTIVE

Pug: The pug is a lot of dog in a very _____ package. It is
ADJECTIVE

known for being loving, outgoing, and _____. And it snores
ADJECTIVE

like a freight _____!
NOUN

Siberian husky: The husky was bred to pull _____ sleds,
ADJECTIVE

and it is known for its _____ endurance and willingness to
ADJECTIVE

_____.
VERB

German shepherd: The German shepherd is not only the most popular

police, guard, and military dog in (the) _____, it is also a
A PLACE

loving family _____.
NOUN

MAD LIBS® is fun to play with friends, but you can also play it by yourself! To begin with, DO NOT look at the story on the page below. Fill in the blanks on this page with the words called for. Then, using the words you have selected, fill in the blank spaces in the story.

Now you've created your own hilarious MAD LIBS® game!

FAMOUS FIDOS: RIN TIN TIN

NOUN _____

PERSON IN ROOM _____

A PLACE _____

VERB _____

CELEBRITY _____

PERSON IN ROOM _____

ADJECTIVE _____

A PLACE _____

NOUN _____

NOUN _____

ADJECTIVE _____

PLURAL NOUN _____

NOUN _____

MAD LIBS®
FAMOUS FIDOS:
RIN TIN TIN

Rin Tin Tin was the biggest movie-star pooch to ever grace the silver

_____. During World War I, Rin Tin Tin's owner and future
　　　NOUN

trainer, _____, discovered the German shepherd puppy on a
　　PERSON IN ROOM

war-torn battlefield in (the) _____. He brought Rin Tin Tin
　　　　　　　　　　　　A PLACE

back to the United States, trained him to _____, and brought
　　　　　　　　　　　　　　　　VERB

him to Hollywood, home to celebrities like _____ and
　　　　　　　　　　　　　　　　　　CELEBRITY

_____. Soon, Rin Tin Tin began to receive _____
PERSON IN ROOM　　　　　　　　　　　　　　　ADJECTIVE

roles in silent films! He quickly became one of the most famous stars

in (the) _____. In 1929, Rin Tin Tin even received the
　　　　A PLACE

most votes for the Academy Award for Best _____—but the
　　　　　　　　　　　　　　　　　NOUN

Academy decided to give the award to a/an _____ instead. All
　　　　　　　　　　　　　　　　　　NOUN

in all, this _____ dog starred in twenty-seven major motion
　　　　ADJECTIVE

_____. He even has his own star on the Hollywood Walk of
PLURAL NOUN

_____!
NOUN

MAD LIBS® is fun to play with friends, but you can also play it by yourself! To begin with, DO NOT look at the story on the page below. Fill in the blanks on this page with the words called for. Then, using the words you have selected, fill in the blank spaces in the story.

Now you've created your own hilarious MAD LIBS® game!

ODE TO THE MUTT

ADJECTIVE _____

PART OF THE BODY _____

PLURAL NOUN _____

PLURAL NOUN _____

PLURAL NOUN _____

NOUN _____

PART OF THE BODY _____

NOUN _____

NOUN _____

A PLACE _____

ANIMAL _____

ADJECTIVE _____

ODE TO THE MUTT

A little bit of this and a little bit of that, the mutt is a/an _____
                                                                    ADJECTIVE

mixed-breed pup that will warm your _____ and chase your
                                        PART OF THE BODY

_____ away. First of all, mutts are just like snowflakes—no two
PLURAL NOUN

_____ are alike! Mutts come in all shapes and _____.
PLURAL NOUN   PLURAL NOUN

Big ones, small ones, fluffy ones, and scruffy ones—there's a mutt for

every _____. Mutts have a special way of worming their way
        NOUN

into your _____. There are millions of mutts in shelters that
          PART OF THE BODY

need your love and _____. They need your love more than the
                    NOUN

average _____, and they'll love you to (the) _____
          NOUN   A PLACE

and back! So next time you are thinking about bringing home a new

_____, consider adopting a/an _____ mutt!
ANIMAL   ADJECTIVE

MAD LIBS® is fun to play with friends, but you can also play it by yourself! To begin with, DO NOT look at the story on the page below. Fill in the blanks on this page with the words called for. Then, using the words you have selected, fill in the blank spaces in the story.

Now you've created your own hilarious MAD LIBS® game!

BEGGING 101

NOUN _____

ADJECTIVE _____

PLURAL NOUN _____

NOUN _____

NOUN _____

PART OF THE BODY (PLURAL) _____

ADJECTIVE _____

PART OF THE BODY (PLURAL) _____

ADVERB _____

ADJECTIVE _____

NOUN _____

TYPE OF FOOD _____

PERSON IN ROOM _____

Are your humans cooking a delicious-smelling _____? Learn
_{NOUN}

to beg like a pro with these _____ tips, and you'll be eating
_{ADJECTIVE}

tasty _____ in no time!
_{PLURAL NOUN}

- Identify the weakest _____ at the dinner table. Who is the
_{NOUN}

  most likely to sneak you a/an _____? Sit as close to that
_{NOUN}

  person as possible.

- Stare up at your target with your biggest, saddest puppy-dog

  _____. If possible, think of something that
_{PART OF THE BODY (PLURAL)}

  makes you feel _____ so you can work up some tears.
_{ADJECTIVE}

- Squint your _____ so you look extra weak and
_{PART OF THE BODY (PLURAL)}

  hungry. Lie down on the ground and pout _____. Basically,
_{ADVERB}

  make yourself look as pathetic and _____ as possible.
_{ADJECTIVE}

- Still not getting any food? Try crying like a/an _____.
_{NOUN}

- If all else fails, grab that delicious _____ with your teeth
_{TYPE OF FOOD}

  and make a run for it—quick! Before _____ catches you!
_{PERSON IN ROOM}

MAD LIBS® is fun to play with friends, but you can also play it by yourself! To begin with, DO NOT look at the story on the page below. Fill in the blanks on this page with the words called for. Then, using the words you have selected, fill in the blank spaces in the story.

Now you've created your own hilarious MAD LIBS® game!

DOGGY DREAMS

ADJECTIVE _____

PART OF THE BODY (PLURAL) _____

ADVERB _____

ADJECTIVE _____

EXCLAMATION _____

VERB ENDING IN "ING" _____

NOUN _____

PART OF THE BODY (PLURAL) _____

EXCLAMATION _____

NOUN _____

SAME NOUN _____

PLURAL NOUN _____

VERB _____

PART OF THE BODY (PLURAL) _____

PLURAL NOUN _____

PERSON IN ROOM _____

PART OF THE BODY _____

ADJECTIVE _____

MAD LIBS®

DOGGY DREAMS

You know what it looks like when your sleeping dog is having a/an

_____ dream: Their tail swishes, their _____
ADJECTIVE   PART OF THE BODY (PLURAL)

twitch, and they bark _____. But what do dogs dream about?
                           ADVERB

Here's one dog's _____ dream:
                    ADJECTIVE

_____! What's that little flash of white fur
EXCLAMATION

_____ in my backyard? It's a bunny _____!
VERB ENDING IN "ING"   NOUN

I have to chase it! I run, run, run, as fast my _____
                                                 PART OF THE BODY (PLURAL)

will carry me. Oh, _____! The bunny has hidden in a/an
                      EXCLAMATION

_____! I sniff the _____, and sure enough, it's in there
NOUN   SAME NOUN

with a den of baby _____! I want to play with them so bad, I
                     PLURAL NOUN

could _____! I bark at the top of my _____.
       VERB   PART OF THE BODY (PLURAL)

Come out and play, you fluffy little _____! But before I can,
                                      PLURAL NOUN

_____ scratches my _____ and wakes me up. It
PERSON IN ROOM   PART OF THE BODY

was all just a/an _____ dream!
                   ADJECTIVE

MAD LIBS® is fun to play with friends, but you can also play it by yourself! To begin with, DO NOT look at the story on the page below. Fill in the blanks on this page with the words called for. Then, using the words you have selected, fill in the blank spaces in the story.

Now you've created your own hilarious MAD LIBS® game!

WHO'S THAT DOG?, PART 2

ADJECTIVE _____

VERB _____

ADJECTIVE _____

ADJECTIVE _____

PART OF THE BODY (PLURAL) _____

ADJECTIVE _____

ADJECTIVE _____

PLURAL NOUN _____

ADJECTIVE _____

PLURAL NOUN _____

NOUN _____

NOUN _____

MAD LIBS

WHO'S THAT DOG?, PART 2

More _____ dog breeds for you to love and _____!
      ADJECTIVE   VERB

Poodle: The curly-haired poodle, best known for its _____
                                                     ADJECTIVE

haircut, is exceptionally smart and _____.
                                       ADJECTIVE

Dachshund: Known for its long body and short _____,
                                      PART OF THE BODY (PLURAL)

the dachshund has a friendly personality and a/an _____ sense
                                                  ADJECTIVE

of smell.

Beagle: This hunting dog is happy-go-_____, friendly, and
                                      ADJECTIVE

loves the company of humans and other _____.
                                           PLURAL NOUN

Great Dane: The gentle Great Dane, famous for its _____
                                              ADJECTIVE

size, is also known as "the king of _____."
                                      PLURAL NOUN

Chihuahua: This sassy little _____, often called a "purse
                                    NOUN

dog," is a big dog in a little _____.
                              NOUN

MAD LIBS® is fun to play with friends, but you can also play it by yourself! To begin with, DO NOT look at the story on the page below. Fill in the blanks on this page with the words called for. Then, using the words you have selected, fill in the blank spaces in the story.

Now you've created your own hilarious MAD LIBS® game!

FAMOUS FIDOS: LASSIE

ADJECTIVE _____

ADJECTIVE _____

A PLACE _____

PERSON IN ROOM (MALE) _____

ADJECTIVE _____

ADJECTIVE _____

VERB _____

ADVERB _____

PERSON IN ROOM (MALE) _____

NOUN _____

NOUN _____

NOUN _____

ADJECTIVE _____

NOUN _____

MAD LIBS

FAMOUS FIDOS: LASSIE

Lassie the collie was famous for her heroics on television and the

_____ screen. On the TV show *Lassie*, the collie lived in
    ADJECTIVE

a/an _____ farming community in (the) _____. Lassie
    ADJECTIVE   A PLACE

belonged to an eleven-year-old boy named _____,
                                    PERSON IN ROOM (MALE)

as well as his mother and _____ grandfather. Whenever the
                          ADJECTIVE

_____ boy got into trouble, Lassie would _____ to
  ADJECTIVE   VERB

the rescue, or she would run and find help. "BARK, BARK!" Lassie

would say _____. "What's that, girl?" the person would ask.
        ADVERB

"Little _____ fell down a/an _____?" Quick
    PERSON IN ROOM (MALE)   NOUN

as a/an _____, the trapped _____ would be safe and
     NOUN   NOUN

_____. And once again, Lassie saved the _____!
  ADJECTIVE   NOUN

MAD LIBS® is fun to play with friends, but you can also play it by yourself! To begin with, DO NOT look at the story on the page below. Fill in the blanks on this page with the words called for. Then, using the words you have selected, fill in the blank spaces in the story.

Now you've created your own hilarious MAD LIBS® game!

HAIL TO THE POOCH

PERSON IN ROOM _____

ADJECTIVE _____

ADJECTIVE _____

PLURAL NOUN _____

TYPE OF FOOD _____

NOUN _____

ADJECTIVE _____

ADJECTIVE _____

NOUN _____

NOUN _____

CELEBRITY _____

NOUN _____

MAD LIBS

HAIL TO THE POOCH

From George Washington to _____ to Barack Obama, many
PERSON IN ROOM

United States presidents have been _____ dog lovers. Here's a
ADJECTIVE

list of _____ First Dogs:
ADJECTIVE

- **Laddie Boy:** Warren G. Harding once invited neighborhood

  _____ to the White House for his Airedale terrier's birthday
  PLURAL NOUN

  party, where they ate _____ made of dog biscuits!
  TYPE OF FOOD

- **Fala:** Franklin Delano Roosevelt's beloved Scottish terrier was

  named after an Army _____ and had his own _____
  NOUN   ADJECTIVE

  secretary. Fala even starred in a/an _____ movie!
  ADJECTIVE

- **Millie:** George H.W. Bush's springer spaniel published her own

  book, ghostwritten by the First _____, which sold more
  NOUN

  copies than President Bush's _____!
  NOUN

- **Bo and Sunny:** Barack Obama received Bo the Portuguese water

  dog as a gift from _____. A few years later, the First Family
  CELEBRITY

  got Sunny, another Portuguese water _____.
  NOUN

MAD LIBS® is fun to play with friends, but you can also play it by yourself! To begin with, DO NOT look at the story on the page below. Fill in the blanks on this page with the words called for. Then, using the words you have selected, fill in the blank spaces in the story.

Now you've created your own hilarious MAD LIBS® game!

CANINE CAREERS

PLURAL NOUN _____

ADJECTIVE _____

PART OF THE BODY _____

A PLACE _____

A PLACE _____

ADJECTIVE _____

PLURAL NOUN _____

PART OF THE BODY (PLURAL) _____

PLURAL NOUN _____

PLURAL NOUN _____

ADJECTIVE _____

ADJECTIVE _____

PART OF THE BODY (PLURAL) _____

PLURAL NOUN _____

MAD LIBS®
CANINE CAREERS

Not all dogs nap and play with their toy _____ all day. Some

PLURAL NOUN

dogs have _____ jobs!

ADJECTIVE

- **Guide dogs:** Guide dogs, or Seeing _____ dogs, help

PART OF THE BODY

  lead the blind where they need to go, like to (the) _____ or

A PLACE

  (the) _____ .

A PLACE

- **Military dogs:** These dogs help troops in _____ military

ADJECTIVE

  missions. They act as guard dogs, looking out for _____ ,

PLURAL NOUN

  and they use their powerful _____ to sniff out

PART OF THE BODY (PLURAL)

  dangerous _____ . US Air Force dogs even jump out of

PLURAL NOUN

  flying _____ with their airmen!

PLURAL NOUN

- **Search-and-rescue dogs:** In a/an _____ disaster or

ADJECTIVE

  in the _____ wilderness, these dogs use their powerful

ADJECTIVE

  _____ to help find missing _____ .

PART OF THE BODY (PLURAL)   PLURAL NOUN

MAD LIBS® is fun to play with friends, but you can also play it by yourself! To begin with, DO NOT look at the story on the page below. Fill in the blanks on this page with the words called for. Then, using the words you have selected, fill in the blank spaces in the story.

Now you've created your own hilarious MAD LIBS® game!

DIVA DOG

ADJECTIVE _____

NOUN _____

PART OF THE BODY _____

SILLY WORD _____

SAME SILLY WORD _____

A PLACE _____

NOUN _____

NOUN _____

NOUN _____

PART OF THE BODY _____

ADJECTIVE _____

VERB ENDING IN "S" _____

ADJECTIVE _____

PART OF THE BODY _____

ADJECTIVE _____

NOUN _____

MAD LIBS®

DIVA DOG

Who's that _____ pooch with the fluffy little _____
       ADJECTIVE   NOUN

and the cute _____? Why, that's Little Miss _____!
          PART OF THE BODY   SILLY WORD

Little Miss _____ is famous throughout (the) _____.
        SAME SILLY WORD   A PLACE

Her _____ is splashed all over the Internet, and in books and
     NOUN

magazines like _____ *Weekly* and *Life &* _____.
           NOUN   NOUN

Little Miss can't go anywhere without someone recognizing her

_____! Luckily, Little Miss likes attention from the
PART OF THE BODY

_____ pup-parazzi. She _____ for the cameras, and
 ADJECTIVE   VERB ENDING IN "S"

greets all her _____ fans with a smile on her _____.
        ADJECTIVE   PART OF THE BODY

After all, without her _____ fans, Little Miss would be just
             ADJECTIVE

another cute face in the _____!
          NOUN

MAD LIBS® is fun to play with friends, but you can also play it by yourself! To begin with, DO NOT look at the story on the page below. Fill in the blanks on this page with the words called for. Then, using the words you have selected, fill in the blank spaces in the story.

Now you've created your own hilarious MAD LIBS® game!

WHO'S THAT DOG?, PART 3

NOUN _____

ADJECTIVE _____

ANIMAL (PLURAL) _____

NOUN _____

NOUN _____

PART OF THE BODY _____

NOUN _____

PART OF THE BODY _____

NOUN _____

PLURAL NOUN _____

VERB ENDING IN "ING" _____

PLURAL NOUN _____

PART OF THE BODY _____

NOUN _____

PLURAL NOUN _____

MAD LIBS

WHO'S THAT DOG?, PART 3

A few more dog breeds to brighten your _____!
<u>NOUN</u>

Yorkshire terrier: Yorkies may be small, but they are brave and

_____. Yorkies were originally bred to hunt _____
<u>ADJECTIVE</u>   <u>ANIMAL (PLURAL)</u>

in _____ factories!
<u>NOUN</u>

Doberman pinscher: The Doberman is a muscular _____.
<u>NOUN</u>

With its intelligent _____ , the Doberman is often trained
<u>PART OF THE BODY</u>

as a police _____.
<u>NOUN</u>

Shih tzu: The shih tzu has a long and luxurious _____. This
<u>PART OF THE BODY</u>

playful _____ is usually friendly toward all _____.
<u>NOUN</u>   <u>PLURAL NOUN</u>

Australian shepherd: Aussies are very energetic and require daily

_____ to be happy. They are great at herding crowds
<u>VERB ENDING IN "ING"</u>

of _____ on the farm.
<u>PLURAL NOUN</u>

Pomeranian: The Pomeranian has a big, fluffy _____ to
<u>PART OF THE BODY</u>

match its outgoing _____. This intelligent little dog loves to
<u>NOUN</u>

please its _____.
<u>PLURAL NOUN</u>

MAD LIBS® is fun to play with friends, but you can also play it by yourself! To begin with, DO NOT look at the story on the page below. Fill in the blanks on this page with the words called for. Then, using the words you have selected, fill in the blank spaces in the story.

Now you've created your own hilarious MAD LIBS® game!

POOCH PALACE

ADJECTIVE _____

ANIMAL _____

NOUN _____

TYPE OF LIQUID _____

ADJECTIVE _____

PART OF THE BODY _____

OCCUPATION _____

NOUN _____

SILLY WORD _____

PART OF THE BODY _____

A PLACE _____

PART OF THE BODY _____

NOUN _____

PLURAL NOUN _____

Welcome to the _____ Pooch Palace, the dog spa for all your
                        ADJECTIVE

grooming needs! Below is our spa menu. How do you want to pamper

your _____ today?
         ANIMAL

- **Paw-dicure:** We'll not only trim your _____ 's nails,
                                              NOUN

    we'll paint them with a coat of _____ so your pup looks
                                      TYPE OF LIQUID

    _____ and stylish.
      ADJECTIVE

- **Pup massage:** If your dog is in need of some rest and relaxation,

    a/an _____ massage might be just what the _____
          PART OF THE BODY   OCCUPATION
    ordered!

- **Doggy 'do:** Is your _____ looking shaggy? Our renowned
                          NOUN

    stylist, Pierre _____, gives the best _____-cut
                     SILLY WORD   PART OF THE BODY

    this side of (the) _____.
                        A PLACE

- **Fur dye:** If you've ever wanted your dog's _____ to
                                                 PART OF THE BODY

    match the color of your favorite _____, look no further.
                                      NOUN

    The Pooch Palace will make all your _____ come true!
                                         PLURAL NOUN

MAD LIBS® is fun to play with friends, but you can also play it by yourself! To begin with, DO NOT look at the story on the page below. Fill in the blanks on this page with the words called for. Then, using the words you have selected, fill in the blank spaces in the story.

Now you've created your own hilarious MAD LIBS® game!

HOMEWARD BOUND

A PLACE _____

ADJECTIVE _____

PERSON IN ROOM (FEMALE) _____

NUMBER _____

VERB (PAST TENSE) _____

PERSON IN ROOM _____

PART OF THE BODY (PLURAL) _____

NOUN _____

ADJECTIVE _____

NOUN _____

NOUN _____

PERSON IN ROOM _____

TYPE OF LIQUID _____

ADJECTIVE _____

HOMEWARD BOUND

In (the) _____ today, one _____ family was reunited
     A PLACE   ADJECTIVE

with their beloved dog, _____, who made her way
               PERSON IN ROOM (FEMALE)

home after being missing for _____ days. "She just showed
                     NUMBER

up on our front doorstep this morning and _____," said
                          VERB (PAST TENSE)

_____. "We couldn't believe our _____."
PERSON IN ROOM   PART OF THE BODY (PLURAL)

The family dog disappeared after leaving the family's front yard to chase

after a wild _____ one afternoon, and the family has been
          NOUN

worried _____ ever since. They put up "lost _____"
      ADJECTIVE   NOUN

posters all over the neighborhood, and even put a/an _____ in
                                   NOUN

the local newspaper. "We have no idea where she's been all this time,"

said _____. "We're just happier than a pig in _____
     PERSON IN ROOM   TYPE OF LIQUID

that she's home again. We can't wait to spoil her _____."
                                      ADJECTIVE

MAD LIBS® is fun to play with friends, but you can also play it by yourself! To begin with, DO NOT look at the story on the page below. Fill in the blanks on this page with the words called for. Then, using the words you have selected, fill in the blank spaces in the story.

Now you've created your own hilarious MAD LIBS® game!

WONDER DOG

VERB _____

ADJECTIVE _____

PART OF THE BODY (PLURAL) _____

ADJECTIVE _____

NOUN _____

PART OF THE BODY _____

VERB ENDING IN "ING" _____

ADJECTIVE _____

PART OF THE BODY (PLURAL) _____

ADVERB _____

NOUN _____

ADJECTIVE _____

PLURAL NOUN _____

ADJECTIVE _____

ADJECTIVE _____

ADVERB _____

VERB _____

MAD LIBS®
WONDER DOG

Lots of dogs can sit, stay, and _____. But not many can do
_____VERB_____

these _____ tricks!
_____ADJECTIVE_____

- **Play dead:** When you say, "Bang! Bang!" some dogs will roll onto

  their _____ and act _____. This act is
  ___PART OF THE BODY (PLURAL)___   ___ADJECTIVE___

  sure to tickle your funny _____.
  _____NOUN_____

- **Dance:** Your dog may know how to wag its _____ to
  _____PART OF THE BODY_____

  the beat, but can it dance like nobody's _____?
  _____VERB ENDING IN "ING"_____

  A dog that knows this _____ trick can stand on its hind
  _____ADJECTIVE_____

  _____ and spin around _____!
  ___PART OF THE BODY (PLURAL)___   ___ADVERB___

- **Bring my slippers:** Feeling lazy and don't want to get out of your

  comfy _____? Ask your dog to do it! If your dog knows
  _____NOUN_____

  this _____ trick, say, "Bring my slippers," and your dog
  _____ADJECTIVE_____

  will bring your _____ to you!
  _____PLURAL NOUN_____

- **Jump rope:** If your dog knows this _____ trick, grab a/an
  _____ADJECTIVE_____

  _____ rope and a partner, swing the rope _____,
  ___ADJECTIVE___   ___ADVERB___

  and your dog will _____ over it again and again!
  _____VERB_____

MAD LIBS® is fun to play with friends, but you can also play it by yourself! To begin with, DO NOT look at the story on the page below. Fill in the blanks on this page with the words called for. Then, using the words you have selected, fill in the blank spaces in the story.

Now you've created your own hilarious MAD LIBS® game!

DOG'S DELIGHT

VERB ENDING IN "S" _____

PART OF THE BODY _____

ADJECTIVE _____

PLURAL NOUN _____

ANIMAL _____

VERB _____

VERB _____

PLURAL NOUN _____

NOUN _____

PLURAL NOUN _____

NOUN _____

NOUN _____

NOUN _____

PLURAL NOUN _____

NOUN _____

ADJECTIVE _____

PART OF THE BODY _____

NOUN _____

MAD LIBS®

DOG'S DELIGHT

You know your dog is happy when it _____ and wags
VERB ENDING IN "S"

its _____ back and forth. If you want your dog to be
PART OF THE BODY

_____ as a clam at all times, try any of the following
ADJECTIVE

_____. It's a countdown of your _____'s favorite things!
PLURAL NOUN   ANIMAL

5. **Walks:** Though some dogs would rather stay home and

_____, most dogs love to go for walks to _____
VERB   VERB

on fire hydrants and sniff _____.
PLURAL NOUN

4. **Naps:** Dogs love to curl up on a/an _____ and dream about
NOUN

_____—especially if they're cuddling with their favorite
PLURAL NOUN

_____.
NOUN

3. **Playtime:** Fidos love to play fetch with a/an _____ or run
NOUN

around chasing a/an _____. Sometimes, _____
NOUN   PLURAL NOUN

just wanna have fun!

2. **Food:** Whether it's a can of dog _____ or _____
NOUN   ADJECTIVE

table scraps, dogs love to eat. The way to a dog's heart is definitely

through its _____!
PART OF THE BODY

1. **You!:** After all, a dog is a/an _____'s best friend.
NOUN

MAD LIBS® is fun to play with friends, but you can also play it by yourself! To begin with, DO NOT look at the story on the page below. Fill in the blanks on this page with the words called for. Then, using the words you have selected, fill in the blank spaces in the story.

Now you've created your own hilarious MAD LIBS® game!

WHO'S THAT DOG?, PART 4

VERB _____

COLOR _____

NOUN _____

VERB ENDING IN "ING" _____

NOUN _____

PART OF THE BODY _____

VERB _____

PART OF THE BODY (PLURAL) _____

A PLACE _____

NUMBER _____

ADJECTIVE _____

VERB _____

ADJECTIVE _____

PLURAL NOUN _____

A PLACE _____

ADJECTIVE _____

MAD LIBS

WHO'S THAT DOG?, PART 4

A final few furry dog breeds for you to love and _____ :
                                                    VERB

Collie: The brown, white, and _____ collie is a friendly family
                                       COLOR

_____ , known for its grace and elegance when _____ .
NOUN   VERB ENDING IN "ING"

Dalmation: This black-and-white _____ is the only dog
                                         NOUN

breed with spots on its _____ . They have lots of energy and
                          PART OF THE BODY

need to _____ a lot.
          VERB

Pembroke Welsh corgi: The corgi is known for its very short

_____ and stout body. The queen of (the)
PART OF THE BODY (PLURAL)

_____ owns _____ corgis!
A PLACE   NUMBER

Miniature schnauzer: The miniature schnauzer may be small, but it is

a/an _____ guard dog, and will _____ at the sign of
       ADJECTIVE   VERB

any _____ intruder.
      ADJECTIVE

St. Bernard: The St. Bernard was originally used to hunt for

_____ during snowstorms in (the) _____ . They are
PLURAL NOUN   A PLACE

very gentle and _____ .
                  ADJECTIVE

MAD LIBS® is fun to play with friends, but you can also play it by yourself! To begin with, DO NOT look at the story on the page below. Fill in the blanks on this page with the words called for. Then, using the words you have selected, fill in the blank spaces in the story.

Now you've created your own hilarious MAD LIBS® game!

LET'S GO FOR A RIDE!

PERSON IN ROOM _____

PART OF THE BODY (PLURAL) _____

PART OF THE BODY (PLURAL) _____

ADJECTIVE _____

NOUN _____

NOUN _____

PART OF THE BODY _____

PLURAL NOUN _____

PART OF THE BODY (PLURAL) _____

PART OF THE BODY _____

ADJECTIVE _____

ADVERB _____

NOUN _____

PERSON IN ROOM _____

EXCLAMATION _____

NOUN _____

MAD LIBS®

LET'S GO FOR A RIDE!

"_____, come!" I hear my owner call out. My
<u>PERSON IN ROOM</u>

_____ perk up—is that the sound of the
<u>PART OF THE BODY (PLURAL)</u>

garage door opening? Suddenly, I am excited from my head to my

_____. Can it be? Am I going for a/an _____
<u>PART OF THE BODY (PLURAL)</u>   <u>ADJECTIVE</u>

car ride? I bound to the door, where I see my owner getting into the car.

She pats the seat. "Come on, _____!" she calls. This is the best
                              <u>NOUN</u>

_____ ever! I hop happily into the front seat and immediately
<u>NOUN</u>

stick my _____ out of the car window. We drive away
         <u>PART OF THE BODY</u>

down the street, passing houses and mailboxes and _____. I
                                                    <u>PLURAL NOUN</u>

can feel the wind in my _____ and the sun on my
                        <u>PART OF THE BODY (PLURAL)</u>

_____, and everything smells _____. *Where are we*
<u>PART OF THE BODY</u>   <u>ADJECTIVE</u>

going? I wonder _____. So you can imagine my _____
                  <u>ADVERB</u>   <u>NOUN</u>

as we pulled into the parking lot of Dr. _____'s office. *We're*
                                         <u>PERSON IN ROOM</u>

going to the vet? _____! This is the worst _____ ever!
                    <u>EXCLAMATION</u>   <u>NOUN</u>

MAD LIBS® is fun to play with friends, but you can also play it by yourself! To begin with, DO NOT look at the story on the page below. Fill in the blanks on this page with the words called for. Then, using the words you have selected, fill in the blank spaces in the story.

Now you've created your own hilarious MAD LIBS® game!

FAMOUS FIDOS: SCOOBY-DOO

NOUN _____

NOUN _____

PERSON IN ROOM (FEMALE) _____

PERSON IN ROOM (MALE) _____

NOUN _____

ADJECTIVE _____

PLURAL NOUN _____

PLURAL NOUN _____

SAME PLURAL NOUN _____

PLURAL NOUN _____

PLURAL NOUN _____

ADJECTIVE _____

SILLY WORD _____

MAD LIBS
FAMOUS FIDOS:
SCOOBY-DOO

Scooby-Doo is the star of the animated television _____ *Scooby-*
                                                    NOUN

Doo, Where Are You! Scooby-Doo, also known as Scooby, is a talking

_____ who solves mysteries along with four teenagers named
NOUN

Shaggy, Daphne, _____, and _____.
                PERSON IN ROOM (FEMALE)   PERSON IN ROOM (MALE)

Scooby-Doo, a Great _____, belongs to his _____
                     NOUN   ADJECTIVE

friend, Shaggy. Much like Shaggy, Scooby is scared of _____
                                                       PLURAL NOUN

and is always hungry for cookies called Scooby _____.
                                                PLURAL NOUN

Luckily, the prospect of eating Scooby _____ and keeping
                                        SAME PLURAL NOUN

his friends safe from _____ helps Scooby to be brave and
                       PLURAL NOUN

stand up to scary _____. Scooby and his friends always solve
                   PLURAL NOUN

the _____ mystery, and Scooby always ends each episode by
     ADJECTIVE

saying " _____-dooby-doo!"
          SILLY WORD

MAD LIBS® is fun to play with friends, but you can also play it by yourself! To begin with, DO NOT look at the story on the page below. Fill in the blanks on this page with the words called for. Then, using the words you have selected, fill in the blank spaces in the story.

Now you've created your own hilarious MAD LIBS® game!

DOGS VERSUS CATS

ADJECTIVE _____

ADJECTIVE _____

PART OF THE BODY _____

NUMBER _____

ADJECTIVE _____

PLURAL NOUN _____

NOUN _____

PLURAL NOUN _____

PART OF THE BODY (PLURAL) _____

NOUN _____

PART OF THE BODY _____

NOUN _____

NOUN _____

NOUN _____

SAME NOUN _____

ADJECTIVE _____

NOUN _____

MAD LIBS®

DOGS VERSUS CATS

Which are better, _____ cats or _____ dogs? Anyone
    ADJECTIVE   ADJECTIVE

with half a/an _____ knows that dogs are _____
              PART OF THE BODY   NUMBER

times better than cats. Dogs are _____ companions, while
                                   ADJECTIVE

cats only care about their own _____. Dogs are loyal to their
                                PLURAL NOUN

_____, but cats will love whoever gives them _____
    NOUN   PLURAL NOUN

to eat. Dogs like to have their _____ rubbed, while
                                PART OF THE BODY (PLURAL)

cats will bite your _____ if you try to put a/an _____
                      NOUN   PART OF THE BODY

on them. Most dogs love going for rides in a/an _____, but
                                                   NOUN

cats just get sick all over your favorite _____. Dogs love to play
                                            NOUN

fetch with a/an _____, but if you throw a/an _____
                   NOUN   SAME NOUN

for a cat, it will just look at you like you're _____. All in all,
                                                  ADJECTIVE

when it comes to dogs versus cats, only the dog is truly man's best

_____.
   NOUN

MAD LIBS® is fun to play with friends, but you can also play it by yourself! To begin with, DO NOT look at the story on the page below. Fill in the blanks on this page with the words called for. Then, using the words you have selected, fill in the blank spaces in the story.

Now you've created your own hilarious MAD LIBS® game!

FOREVER HOME

LAST NAME _____

NOUN _____

ADJECTIVE _____

ADJECTIVE _____

PART OF THE BODY (PLURAL) _____

COLOR _____

PART OF THE BODY _____

ADJECTIVE _____

NOUN _____

A PLACE _____

ADJECTIVE _____

PLURAL NOUN _____

ADJECTIVE _____

ADJECTIVE _____

PART OF THE BODY _____

EXCLAMATION _____

ADVERB _____

MAD LIBS®

FOREVER HOME

When the _____ family went to the animal shelter,

LAST NAME

they never knew they'd find a/an _____ like Rex. The family

NOUN

looked at all the dogs before making this very _____ decision.

ADJECTIVE

Sure, the puppies were cute and _____, but one older dog

ADJECTIVE

stole the family's _____. His name was Rex, and

PART OF THE BODY (PLURAL)

with his fuzzy _____ fur, his crooked _____, and

COLOR — PART OF THE BODY

his _____ personality, the family knew they'd found their new

ADJECTIVE

_____. Plus, by bringing Rex back to (the) _____

NOUN — A PLACE

with them, they saved his life. Now Rex would have a/an _____

ADJECTIVE

place to sleep, _____ to eat, and a/an _____ family

PLURAL NOUN — ADJECTIVE

to call his own. And Rex would more than repay his family with lots of

_____ wet kisses on the _____ and unconditional

ADJECTIVE — PART OF THE BODY

love. _____! Rex had found his forever home, and they all

EXCLAMATION

lived _____ ever after.

ADVERB

Download Mad Libs today!

Join the millions of Mad Libs fans creating
wacky and wonderful stories on our apps!